Working Together Against
HOMELESSNESS

Homelessness is an international problem.

❖The Library of Social Activism❖

Working Together Against

HOMELESSNESS

**Eugene Hurwitz
and Sue Hurwitz**

THE ROSEN PUBLISHING GROUP, INC.
NEW YORK

In Memory of Our Parents Dorothy and Sol Botwin and
Fanny and Sam Hurwitz

Published in 1994 by The Rosen Publishing Group, Inc.
29 East 21st Street, New York, NY 10010

First Edition

Library of Congress Cataloging-in-Publication Data

Hurwitz, Eugene.
    Working together against homelessness / by Eugene Hurwitz and
Sue Hurwitz. — 1st ed.
      p.   cm. — (The Library of social activism)
    Includes bibliographical references and index.
    ISBN 0-8239-1772-X
    1. Homelessness—United States—Juvenile literature. 2. Homeless
persons—Services for—United States—Juvenile literature. 3. Youth
volunteers in social service—United States—Juvenile literature.
[1. Homelessness. 2. Homeless persons. 3. Voluntarism.
4. Social action.] I. Hurwitz, Sue, 1934– .
II. Title. III. Series.
HV4504.H87   1994
362.5'8'0973—dc20   94-1022
                                                     CIP
                                                     AC

Manufactured in the United States of America

Contents

INTRODUCTION

WHO ARE THE PEOPLE SLEEPING AND LIVING IN public places? Why are they homeless?

People become homeless for different reasons. Usually, they cannot pay for housing. People with little education and few job skills cannot earn much money. With low incomes, they stay poor. As housing costs rise, more and more poor people cannot afford homes. Around thirteen million children in America live in poverty. At any given time nearly 200,000 children are homeless.

Health problems and job layoffs also keep people from working steadily. Sometimes relatives or friends are able to help until the poor find work. But without help, poor people often become homeless.

Many of our new homeless are women and children. A high rate of divorce, and fathers abandoning families, leave women and children with little or no money. There are also many

Homelessness affects people of all generations.

teen-age mothers raising their children without help. Often, these one-parent families are poor.

People other than the poor become homeless. Some women and children leave home because of physical abuse. Teenage runaways often live on the streets. Alcohol and drug abusers, and the mentally ill, are often homeless. Disabled people who cannot work may become homeless. Some criminals and thieves live on the streets. Illegal immigrants and migrant workers are often homeless.

All the countries of the world have homeless people. It is estimated that nearly 1.2 billion people worldwide live in poverty. That is nearly one fourth of the world's population. About 160 million children under the age of five live in poverty in Third World countries.

Famines cause many people to wander from home in search of food. They become homeless. Wars leave millions of people homeless. Since 1986, more than twenty million people around the world became homeless because of war.

Natural disasters occur all over the world. The 1989 San Francisco earthquake is an example of a natural disaster. So is Hurricane Andrew, the one that hit Florida in 1992. Many thousands of people needed emergency food and shelter.

Many countries cannot help their victims when a natural disaster strikes. That is why people worldwide must pitch in to help.

No one knows how many homeless people there are all over the world, or in America. Since the homeless often move from place to place, they are difficult to count. Many countries do not even try to count their homeless people.

Some people think there may be as many as three million homeless people in America today. Others say there are as few as 350 thousand.

Society must help the homeless, whatever their number might be. Government services do not do enough. Private groups and volunteers must also help. We must all work together to fight homelessness.

All homeless people suffer from physical

and emotional hazards caused by their living conditions. They need help to get their lives back in order.

The homeless need food and clothing. They need low-cost housing. They need health services, both physical and mental. They need job skills to get and keep better paying jobs. They need help to become permanent members of communities. They need help to become self-sufficient.

This book describes some social services our government has provided in the past. It describes some social services offered worldwide and in the U.S.A. today. It describes services that are still needed.

This book also discusses how you can help the homeless. It demonstrates how you can make a difference. It tells you how you can help make society better for everyone. It shows how a better society can begin with you!

❖ **QUESTIONS TO ASK YOURSELF** ❖

Homelessness is an international problem that affects everyone. Here are three ways to think about how it might affect you. 1) Do you know of any homeless people? What do you think are the indications that someone is homeless? 2) Are there homeless people in your town or city? What do you think are some causes of homelessness? 3) Why are you interested in helping the homeless?

Anyone can become homeless.

chapter

1

WHY SHOULD WE CARE ABOUT HOMELESSNESS?

CAN YOU IMAGINE HAVING NOTHING TO EAT OR no safe place to sleep? How would your life change if a natural disaster left you homeless?

Change is a condition of life. But not all change is for the better. No one is immune to economic misfortune. No one is immune to natural disasters. Any of us could become homeless.

Homelessness wears down a person's mind and body. Surviving one more day becomes the focus of a homeless person's life. Worrying about food and shelter leaves people feeling hopeless and helpless. They become too stressed to look for work or for housing.

Homelessness robs people of a normal life. It robs people of all ages of being and feeling safe and secure. Some homeless children have never felt safe or secure. The victims of homelessness feel different from other members of society.

Private groups and individuals have always

American Marine troops were sent to Somalia to help resolve problems that are resulting in starving and homeless children, such as this child in a Somali orphanage.

For decades, people have volunteered their time to help the homeless.

played an important role in helping others less fortunate than themselves. When people volunteer their time or their money to help others, they also benefit. Some people volunteer because "it is the right thing to do". Some people volunteer because helping others makes them feel good about themselves. Some people volunteer because they want to "give something back to society".

Today, private organizations supported by individual contributions account for more than a third of the aid for homeless Americans. Some of these organizations are The United Way, The Salvation Army, and The American Red Cross. Many charitable organizations are funded by churches and synagogues and are run by volunteers.

Homelessness is a social problem. Homelessness is a reflection of the way a society cares for its citizens. As members of society, we have an obligation to help make society better.

❖ QUESTIONS TO ASK YOURSELF ❖

There are many issues attached to the problem of homelessness. Let's think about some of these issues. 1) How do you think people are affected by being homeless? 2) What are some groups doing to help the homeless? 3) If homelessness is a reflection of how a society cares for its citizens, how does your society measure up?

chapter

2

HELP FOR THE HOMELESS

THERE HAS BEEN HOMELESSNESS IN AMERICA since colonial days. In the past, many of the homeless people were single men. Some of these men were alcoholics. They usually traveled from place to place to find temporary work and shelter.

Homeless people who were old or disabled received charity. There were also people who had no money, but were healthy. These people were considered lazy. Often, they were whipped or thrown into prison. Sometimes they were forced to work as servants or farm hands.

In the early 1800s, shelters for the homeless were called "poorhouses." Poorhouses were paid for, or funded, by the local communities. Men, women, and children could find shelter and a little food in poorhouses. In return, they were forced to work long hours farming, cooking, and sewing. Poorhouses were harsh places that did little to help people better themselves.

By the 1850s, settlement houses had replaced poor-houses. Settlement houses were temporary shelters funded by charitable organizations and donations from the rich. Settlement houses helped families start over. They provided job training, and nurseries for the children of working mothers. They offered classes in reading and writing to poor people. The ability to read and write is called literacy. These classes also taught English to the thousands of immigrants flooding into America. With a better education they were able to get better jobs.

Hundreds of thousands of Americans became homeless in the 1930s. After the Stock Market Crash of 1929, many businesses failed, and workers lost their jobs through no fault of their own. This contributed to the Great Depression of the 1930s. Americans faced one of the worst economic crises in our history during the Great Depression.

In addition to this, in the mid-1930s, the Great Plains states suffered a drought. Many fertile farms in Middle America dried up and the land turned into a "dust bowl." Farms failed and those farmers left home to look for work. Often, they became migrant workers and had to move from state to state to keep working. They and their families became homeless.

Locally-funded organizations such as Goodwill, and religious groups, helped the

Unemployment soared during the depression and is on the rise today, contributing to the problem of homelessness.

poor and the homeless. But the huge numbers of people needing help overwhelmed local programs.

Our federal government started funding nationwide programs to help the poor and the homeless. President Franklin Delano Roosevelt (FDR) began his "New Deal" programs in the 1930s. Millions of jobs were created by the government, and people went to work, repairing and extending roads, repairing bridges, and building dams. Many people left homeless began to get back on their feet.

Some of the New Deal programs still function today. Social Security was a New Deal program created to help the poor, the elderly, and the disabled. Social Security, is *not* a welfare program. Social Security is a government pension plan. All working people pay into it, on a regular basis. Only those who pay into it, can receive its benefits.

Other programs established the minimum wage and created still more federal jobs. Government funds supported public housing. These low-rent apartments helped many people into affordable homes.

In the mid-1940s, with the end of World War II the American economy continued to expand. There was work for people. The Great Depression was over. In the 1960s, President Lyndon Johnson launched a "War on Poverty."

Food stamps are issued to the needy in an effort to combat poverty and hunger.

The amount of government money spent on
social welfare programs increased. Medicare and
Medicaid were started, to provide health care
for the poor and the elderly. Other government
programs included the food stamp program
and AFDC (Aid to Families with Dependent
Children). The U.S. Department of Housing
and Urban Development (HUD) provided low-
income housing.

The Stuart B. McKinney Homeless Assist-
ance Act has provided billions of federal dollars
for homeless programs since 1977. These programs included emergency shelter, food, and
health care, both physical and mental. Educa-
tional programs and job training were also
established.

In 1979, the Vietnam Veterans Readjustment
Act was started to help American soldiers who
fought in Vietnam. Some soldiers could not find
work when they returned home. They became
homeless. Today, about one third of our homeless men in the US are Vietnam veterans.

During the 1980s, the federal government
spent less money on social welfare programs.
The American economy also slowed down.
Homelessness began growing steadily in the
1980s and continues to grow in the 1990s.

Present federal programs do give some help
to the homeless. But they do not meet the needs
of the large number of homeless Americans.

Today, about one third of homeless men in the US are Vietnam Veterans.

Help from private citizens and private institutions is also necessary both locally and nationally. Worldwide help for the homeless is crucial.

❖ INTERNATIONAL SOCIAL SERVICES ❖

Refugees are people who flee to a different country to escape war, death, or natural disasters. Refugees form the largest groups of homeless people worldwide.

Refugees usually cannot return to their native countries. Wars, hurricanes, floods, earthquakes or other natural disasters destroy everything these people once owned. They often become permanently displaced or homeless. For example, more than three million refugees have been uprooted and displaced by war in Sudan (Africa) since the 1980s. Many victims of this civil war are still homeless.

Large numbers of refugees are women and children. Most refugees are crowded into camps with little or no sanitation. Medical supplies and food are scarce. These people suffer from malnutrition and starvation. Diseases, including measles, malaria, and tuberculosis, are common in refugee camps. Millions of babies and young children die from diarrhea.

Many of today's refugees come from Afghanistan, Cambodia, Ethiopia, Iran, Iraq, and Nicaragua. Other recent refugees have been displaced from Somalia, Sudan, the former Soviet Union, and Vietnam.

Refugees from the Persian Gulf War of 1991 fled from Kuwait and Iraq. In 1992, Muslim refugees from the former Yugoslavia left Bosnia-Herzegovina to escape the attacks of the Serbian Army.

In 1946, after World War II, The United Nations International Children's Emergency Fund (UNICEF) was established to help children in Europe and China. Today, UNICEF provides emergency help to children in the least developed nations (Third World countries). UNICEF seeks to protect children from death caused by disease, malnutrition, or disasters.

The U.S. Committee for Refugees (USCR) is a nonprofit, nongovernmental organization. This committee reviews and evaluates the plight of refugees and displaced people worldwide. The USCR works closely with the United Nations, and makes recommendations for aid to refugees.

The United Nations Relief Agency and the United Nations High Commissioner for Refugees monitor the conditions of refugees. Both agencies airlift food and supplies into countries at war to help refugees.

The Office of the United Nations High Commissioner for Refugees (UNHCR) helps refugees who have legal and political problems. The UNHCR returns refugees to their homelands or

Immigrant families face obstacles to finding employment and housing.

helps resettle them in other countries. The UNHCR also helps refugees obtain jobs and social benefits.

The International Red Cross coordinates emergency relief after natural disasters in America, and also worldwide. The International Committee of the Red Cross (ICRC) is neutral in times of conflict. This committee provides food and medical supplies and inspects prisoner-of-war camps.

The Salvation Army and the United Way also offer help worldwide, after natural disasters.

There are hundreds of other worthwhile organizations that provide relief for refugees and try to eliminate hunger worldwide. But they cannot reach everyone. Everyone should be concerned because poverty is so widespread all around the world.

We all need to do and give whatever we can. We need to be knowledgeable. We need to be vocal. We need to help develop programs to end suffering worldwide. We can only do this by caring enough to become involved.

❖ QUESTIONS TO ASK YOURSELF ❖

Aid for the homeless comes from many areas. Let's explore two of these possible areas. 1) What government programs are you aware of that help the homeless? 2) What programs are available for homeless refugees?

chapter

3

HOW SOME PEOPLE HELP MAKE A DIFFERENCE

"*DO YOU HELP OUT AT THIS SOUP KITCHEN everyday?*" *Mitch, a fourteen-year-old from the suburbs, asked the worker beside him.*

Lorenzo nodded. He dipped a ladle of beans and filled a small bowl. After placing it on a homeless person's tray he glanced at Mitch.

"My priest says it is important for Latins to be active in programs for the homeless," Lorenzo answered. "Many Spanish-speaking people do not know English. They do not know where to go for help. We need to be around to translate when necessary." Lorenzo shrugged, then he smiled. "Besides, my family was homeless once. I remember how good it was to meet someone who understood."

"No kidding!" Mitch said. He piled a turkey sandwich on the tray pushed up to him. "What happened?"

"It is a long story," Lorenzo answered. "When we get our break, I'll tell you about it."

Later, Lorenzo and Mitch left the serving line and sat down at a table.

"Papa came here from Mexico in the late 1970s as a young man. He was an illegal alien. He could not get a green card." Lorenzo took a sip of water. "Do you know what a green card is?"

Mitch smiled. He placed his water glass on the table. "Sure, a green card is a Resident Alien Card. It certifies that an alien has permanent resident status."

"Right!" Lorenzo glanced at his watch. They had five minutes left before they needed to return to the serving line. "Papa couldn't afford to buy fake documents, so he was doomed to low-paying jobs. He worried constantly about getting caught and sent back to Mexico.

"After Papa and Mama married, they both worked as farm hands. They moved from place to place to follow the crop harvests. From the time I was born, I traveled with them."

Lorenzo became silent. He chose his words very carefully. "Both Papa and Mama worked very hard, long hours. Then Papa hurt his back and he couldn't work. Since they were illegals, they could not get benefits. We lived in our car until our savings ran out.

"Papa felt humiliated that he could not support us. He became depressed and he left us to look for work in another city. Mama and I went to a shelter for homeless women. Mama and I would have starved if it weren't for soup kitchens!

"Mama had no green card, either. After a few

Millions of low income families live in substandard, overcrowded tenements.

months she found a job as a nanny. The family she worked for gave us room and board and we left the shelter. I was able to go to school and our lives became more normal. But, of course, we both missed Papa."

"Is your father with you now?" Mitch asked.

"Yes. We got our lives back together in 1986. A new Immigration Reform and Control Act was passed. It gave undocumented aliens who were living in the U.S. before 1982 a chance to become legal residents. Both Mama and Papa are U.S. citizens now. They both have good jobs. I was born here. I am a U.S. citizen by birth."

"I'm glad everything worked out for you," Mitch said. "I understand why you help out at the soup kitchen so often."

"Why do you work here?" Lorenzo asked his new friend.

"My religious youth group also encourages us to volunteer for worthy causes," Mitch explained. "I feel lucky that my family has a home and enough food. I want to help others who are not so lucky!"

Lorenzo looked around. "Well, you've come to the right place. Homeless people need all the help they can get!"

Mitch looked at Lorenzo, as both boys pushed their chairs back, and got to their feet. "My youth group collects coats and clothing from people who call to donate them. Do you want to join us this weekend?"

"Sure," Lorenzo answered. "Now that I'm eighteen I can use the family car whenever I want to," he said proudly. "Can you use an extra vehicle?"

"Count on it," Mitch said, as both boys headed back to the serving line. "An extra person and an extra car will help tremendously!"

❖ STUDENTS VOLUNTEER ❖

"All right," Claireese began. "Let's get our projects rolling!"

"Mrs. Quinn gave us the whole grading period to work on this," Marybeth complained. "We don't need to work our fingers to the bone now!"

Claireese tightened her lips. "Listen up, Marybeth. Social action is not something you put off until it fits into your schedule. We need to act, and we need to act now!"

"I agree with Claireese," David chimed in. "It may take several months to get answers to our letters. We need to get organized."

"David is right!" Tyler agreed. "I think we should start by getting information about homelessness. Let's write to the National Coalition for the Homeless."

"Any objections?" Claireese asked, looking around the group. When no hands went up, Claireese continued. "We'll write the letter now. We can find the address in our social action guide book! We'll call them first, and ask the name of the person we should write to."

"Good letters are short and simple," David reminded the group. "All we need to do is explain the type of information we want. We don't need to write our entire life stories!"

About thirty minutes later, Claireese read the group's completed letter:

> Claireese Jones
> c/o Mrs. Quinn
> Sixtrees Middle School
> Sixtrees, OH 24680

Name of person (Mr. or Ms.)
National Coalition for the Homeless
1612 K Street, NW, #1004
Washington, DC 20006
Subject: information about homelessness.

Dear Mr. or Ms.:

We are a group of eighth grade students who want to learn more about homelessness and some of its causes.

We want to learn what is being done about it and what we can do to help.

We would appreciate any free information you can send us.

Sincerely,

*Claireese Jones   Marybeth Hunt   DAVID LANDS   Tyler Webb
Bonnie Bernard   Mara Green   Ricky Raven*

Claireese Jones, Marybeth Hunt,
David Lands, Tyler Webb, Bonnie Bernard,
Mara Green, Ricky Raven

Nearly two months later, Mrs. Quinn handed Claireese a thick envelope from the National Coalition for the Homeless. It contained several fact sheets and pamphlets.

"I'm pleased that your group has been busy," Mrs. Quinn said. "Have you contacted any other organizations?"

"Yes," Claireese reported. "We wrote to UNICEF for information on worldwide homelessness. We also wrote to the National Network of Runaway and Youth Services, Inc. for information. We haven't heard from them yet but I'm sure we will."

Mrs. Quinn nodded.

"We will read and discuss this information," Claireese said. "Then our group will submit proposals for the actions we decide to take."

"That's a good idea," said Mrs. Quinn. "I'm anxious to see what you all decide."

During the next week, Claireese's group received responses to their other two letters. Each member of the group read the letters thoroughly. They discussed them at their next group meeting.

"I want to write letters to express my concern about programs for the homeless," Ricky announced. "I'll write to our Congresspersons and Senators. I'll write to our state governor. I'll write to the U.S. Committee for Refugees, also."

"Okay," Claireese agreed. "Get your proposal ready for Mrs. Quinn. We'll need it by next week."

"Your letters will be more impressive if you include a petition," David suggested. *"Marybeth, do you want to help me prepare some petitions to include with Ricky's letters?"*

"What is a petition?" Marybeth asked cautiously. *"A petition is a formal written request. It is often signed by other people who agree with you,"* David explained. *"Our petition would state that we feel more low-income housing is needed for the homeless."*

"More social welfare programs are needed, too," Marybeth added.

"Good point! We will include that, also." David began writing. *"We will pass this around at lunch time. We should have plenty of signatures in a couple of days."* David glanced at Ricky. *"Do you want to include our petitions with your letters?"*

"Of course," Ricky agreed. *"These officials have the power to make a difference. Petitions will let them know that many of us are concerned about homelessness."*

"Some of our teachers would probably like to sign the petition also," Bonnie added. *"Don't forget to ask them to sign."*

"I'd like to help get signatures for our petition, David," Marybeth finally agreed. *"We can ask our parents to sign, too."*

After David finished writing the petition, the students signed it. The document read:

Many celebrities, like the late Audrey Hepburn, work to end homelessness and poverty.

PETITION

We feel that homeless people around the world have a right to affordable housing. They need social services; such as help with obtaining food, medical care, and job training. Governments have an obligation to care for their citizens.

We, the undersigned, would like to see homeless people worldwide receive more support.

Marybeth Hunt
Marybeth Hunt

Ricky Raven
Ricky Raven

DAVID LANDS
David Lands

Mara Green
Mara Green

Tyler Webb
Tyler Webb

Bonnie Bernard
Bonnie Bernard

Claireese Jones
Claireese Jones

"That's good," said Tyler. "The petitions and letters will make a difference. They will show our officials that people care about homelessness."

"What are you going to do for your project?" Claireese asked Tyler.

"I'm going to get volunteers to raise money for the homeless," Tyler said. "I'll run a car-washing day. I'll ask some of my softball team members to donate two afternoons to help."

"How are you going to advertise?" David wanted to know.

"Do you have any suggestions?" Tyler asked.

"You should write a press release and mail it to the newspapers." David thought for a minute. "You should probably use flyers, too."

"I'll be glad to help you with the flyers," Marybeth volunteered. "I love to block print with color markers. The flyers need to be attractive, you know!"

"You got it," Tyler accepted. "Does anyone want to help distribute the flyers?"

"I'll take a big batch to the supermarket and ask them to display the flyers at the checkout counters," Claireese said. "I'll also ask merchants at the mall to tape flyers to their windows."

"That should give us a lot of publicity," Tyler said. "Thanks, I appreciate the help."

"What will you say on the flyer?" Marybeth asked.

"The usual 'W' information. Who, What, When, Where, and Why."

"Give us an example," Marybeth prodded.

Tyler jotted down a few ideas. The sample flyer read:

Concerned Students of Sixtrees Middle
School Social Action Group.

CAR WASH
To raise money for the homeless.
Saturday—whatever date we decide on—
11:00 to 4:00 PM
SIXTREES MIDDLE SCHOOL PARKING LOT

Public figures and celebrities often play a large role in benefits to help the homeless.

"You'll have to get permission to use the school lot before you design the final flyer," Claireese reminded Tyler.

"I'm sure that won't be a problem," he answered.

"What will you do with the money?"

"We'll take it to one of the homeless shelters. They can use it to buy supplies."

"Do you want to volunteer with me to babysit at the Salvation Army?" Bonnie asked, turning to Mara. "I'm going to work in their nursery school on Saturdays."

"Definitely!" Mara answered. "I love little kids. Mom and I knitted afghans for babies all winter. We have seven ready to donate! I'll bring them along."

"That will be a big help!" Bonnie exclaimed. "Most of the kids' moms are single parents. Their paychecks don't go very far. I'm sure your afghans will be put to good use."

"What's your project?" Ricky asked Claireese.

Claireese grinned. "Well, you all know how I like to talk! I'm going to volunteer one day each weekend at a Covenant House. I'll talk to runaway kids who call in on the hotline."

"Remember to listen," Marybeth instructed. "Runaway kids are lonely. They are usually abused. Sometimes they are addicted to drugs. They call a hotline to get help, not to hear idle chatter."

"Give me a break," Claireese said. "All volunteers get training on how to handle calls. I'll say whatever I'm supposed to say!"

Literacy programs teach the critical skills of reading and writing.

"Let's get started," Ricky interrupted. "We need to get our projects approved by Mrs. Quinn. Then we can get to work!"

❖ TUTORING AT A SHELTER ❖

Cris and her brother, Kyle, tutor at a United Way shelter for the homeless Wednesdays after school.

Cris, who is fifteen, tutors Vanessa, who is also fifteen. Vanessa is a single parent whose child has been placed in foster care. Cris is tutoring Vanessa so she can get her general equivalency diploma.

"Did you have any problems with the homework?" Cris asked Vanessa, one Wednesday.

"I got it done. My social worker thinks a GED will help me get a job," Vanessa reminded Cris. "After I get a job I'll have the possibility of getting my daughter back."

Vanessa sat on a mattress in the crowded, noisy room that she shared with three other women. "It is hard to think in a place like this. But I'm going to get out of here. I messed up my life before, but I'm going to get that GED if it kills me."

"You're doing good work, Vanessa," Cris said. "You should have no trouble getting a GED if you keep working this hard." Cris smiled across the mattress, at her new friend. "How is the baby? Did you see her this week?"

After a brief conversation about her child, Vanessa pulled her math homework out. The girls went over the problems, and then Cris explained the new lesson.

In another part of the shelter, Kyle tutored Bobby with his reading. Because his family moved so often, Bobby missed a lot of school. Although he was eleven years old, he was in the third grade. He read at a first grade reading level. Bobby hated school because he could only be with kids his age at recess.

"How was your week?" Kyle asked as he walked with Bobby to the front hall.

"Gross, as usual!" Bobby grumbled. "I can't wait until Dad finds a job and gets us out of here."

"Did you look over the comics I brought last time?"

Volunteer organizations serve hot food to the homeless.

"Yeah." Bobby shrugged. "But someone stole them."

"I brought two more comics today. After we finish our lesson, I'll read them to you."

"I don't want to practice with your flash cards," Bobby said. "I don't need to know how to read."

"Sure you do," Kyle insisted. "You need to know how to read, in order to shop, or to ride a bus. You need to read ingredients on food labels and directions on medicine bottles. You need to read to get a driver's license. You need to read the newspaper to find jobs that are advertised. People who cannot read are at a big disadvantage."

"My dad doesn't read and he gets by," Bobby said. "Besides, reading is boring."

"You'll enjoy reading after you read better," Kyle responded. "Soon, you'll be glad you made the effort to learn."

"What comics did you bring?" Bobby reached over to flip through Kyle's notebook.

"After our lesson, my friend," Kyle opened his box of word cards. "We've got something more important to do first!"

"How did your lesson go?" Kyle asked Cris on the ride home.

"Good," Cris answered. "Vanessa is working hard to turn her life around. I know that isn't easy in her circumstances. I feel good about helping her do it. I admire her courage and determination."

"Bobby still has a problem with his attitude, but I think he's improving, too. He really enjoys listening to me read comics to him. I think he'll want to try to read them by himself soon."

❖ STARTING A VOLUNTEER YOUTH CORPS ❖

Tammy and her brother, Tyrone, saw a TV program about homelessness. "I didn't know that homelessness was so widespread," Tammy remarked. "I'd really like to do something to help homeless people!"

"Does your middle school sponsor a social action group?" Tyrone asked.

"I'm not sure," Tammy replied. "I'll ask tomorrow." She flicked off the commercial at the end of the program. "Does your high school sponsor a group to help the homeless?"

"I don't know," Tyrone admitted. "But I'll check on that tomorrow, too."

After school the following day, Tyrone and Tammy compared information.

"One of our social studies teachers sponsors a volunteer group that earns money to help the needy," Tammy said. "She would like to include the homeless, too. She asked me to find out how to expand the volunteer group."

"That's great!" Tyrone exclaimed. Besides helping the homeless, belonging to the group should be fun."

Tammy sighed. "I really don't know where to begin," she confessed. "Did you find anything out that might help me?"

Tyrone smiled. Our school has a youth group that raises funds for the homeless and helps clean up the grounds around several shelters."

"Are you going to join the volunteer group?"

"You bet! A friend told me that the middle school hasn't organized a group yet. Ashley suggested that you call the Points of Light Foundation to get help in starting one."

"Ashley? Let me guess. You've already become an active member of the high school youth group! What's the number of the Points of Light Foundation?"

Tyrone handed Tammy a slip of paper with the 1–800 number of the national organization.

Tammy took the number and walked to the phone. She was anxious to find out how she could

Many people think that the government should provide affordable housing to people with low or no income.

help others less fortunate than herself. She could hardly wait to take some positive action!

❖ QUESTIONS TO ASK YOURSELF ❖

There are many ways in which you can take positive action. Following are questions to help you come up with some suggestions. 1) Can you name some local groups or organizations working to help the homeless? What are these groups doing? 2) What projects can you and your class develop to help the homeless or help educate others about this problem?

chapter

4

EVERYONE HAS RIGHTS

HOMELESS PEOPLE HAVE BASIC HUMAN RIGHTS just like other citizens.

The Universal Declaration of Human Rights was adopted by the United Nations in 1948. This document set out economic and political rights for all persons worldwide. It established a model for equal protection of all persons under the law, protection against cruel or unusual punishment, and freedom of expression. It states that everyone has the right to an adequate standard of living. This means good housing, clothing, medical care, and food.

Private charities, organizations and volunteers provide much of the help for America's homeless. But this is temporary help. Only government-funded programs can provide permanent solutions for homelessness.

Many Americans receive government help. People get personal deductions on their federal income tax. Large corporations receive large tax

Homeless people have basic human rights just like everyone else.

deductions for locating their companies in certain areas. Farmers get low-interest loans and government money to support prices. Don't the homeless deserve to have their rights honored?

Homelessness cannot be eliminated overnight. More funding for social welfare programs is necessary. Low-income housing, job training, education, and health benefits should be supported by government programs.

Still, private citizens can give a lot of temporary help. You don't need to be rich or famous to do your share. All you need is the desire to help and the determination to act on it.

❖ QUESTIONS TO ASK YOURSELF ❖

There are two kinds of solutions to homelessness: temporary and permanent. Let's explore both kinds. 1) Can you think of some temporary solutions? 2) Who can provide permanent solutions? 3) What must be done to eliminate homelessness?

chapter

5

WHAT YOU CAN DO TO HELP

LEARN ABOUT THE NEEDS OF THE HOMELESS. Check books out of your library. Contact sources listed in the appendix of this book.

Help the homeless by publicizing their needs. Encourage your school or religious group to sponsor lectures given by advocates for the homeless. Write letters to the editors of your newspapers asking for more coverage on homelessness.

Organize events at your school, club, or religious group to earn money to donate to the homeless. Popular fundraisers include chili dinners, pancake breakfasts, and auctions. Group trips to sports events or the theater, or raffles, can also raise funds.

Persuade your peers to help you earn money for the homeless. Sponsoring walkathons, washing cars, mowing lawns, having a bake sale or a carnival, are projects that most young adults enjoy. Such events publicize the needs of the homeless and raise the awareness of others.

Distribute flyers, mail news releases, and ask for free radio announcements, to publicize your events. Ask businesses to provide discount coupons which can be given to those who contribute to your fundraisers.

Participate in food and clothing drives sponsored by schools, the Boy Scouts, Girl Scouts, religious groups, or clubs. Take outgrown clothing or canned goods to a homeless shelter on your own, or with a friend.

Support the homeless by writing letters to your representatives in government. Adapt the sample letter forms in the appendix. You are future voters, your views will influence your representatives.

Remember, you can make a difference!

On a global level, it is estimated that by the end of this century, more than one half of all people will live in cities. This means that many more cities of the world will face poverty, unemployment, and homelessness on a very large scale.

The twenty-three cities considered to be the largest, or "mega cities," are New York and Los Angeles, USA; Mexico City, Mexico; Rio de Janeiro, and São Paulo, Brazil; Buenos Aires, Argentina; London, England; Moscow, Russia; Beijung, Tianjin, and Shanghai, China; Seoul Korea; Tokyo, Japan; Calcutta, Delhi, and Bombay, India; Karachi, Pakistan; Dacca, Bangladesh; Bangkok, Thailand; Manila, Phillipines; Jakarta, Indonesia; Lagos, Nigeria.

The mega-cities named on the previous page will each have more than ten million people.

At this time, the two cities whose problems are most pronounced, are New York and Los Angeles.

Urban (city) leaders from these twenty-three cities have come together to form partnerships between the public, private, and voluntary sectors (parts) of society. They believe that we must all work together to make our cities centers of hope and opportunity. These leaders say that we, the people, must be the ones to work towards workable, livable cities.

They formed an organization called the MEGA-CITIES PROJECT and recently had their Seventh Annual Global Coordinators' Meeting, in Jakarta, Indonesia. There, they shared information on new ideas, worked on the further development of the global network, and also committed themselves to work with the United Nations. We can all make a difference.

❖ QUESTIONS TO ASK YOURSELF ❖

You must learn about the problem to be a part of the solution. Let's think about some ways to learn about and help solve homelessness. 1) How can you learn more about the needs of the homeless? 2) Why do you think homelessness is more prevalent in cities than in small towns or rural areas? 3) What kinds of events can you and your class organize to raise money for the homeless?

VOLUNTEER ORGANIZATIONS YOU CAN CALL

MANY AGENCIES REQUIRE THAT VOLUNTEERS BE at least eighteen years old. Others require that they be at least twenty-one. This is because of insurance requirements.

Some agencies will use younger volunteers if they are part of a group supervised by a person over twenty-one. For this reason, it is easier to volunteer through a church or school group.

If your school or religious group do not sponsor activities to help the homeless, there are several agencies you can call.

Points of Light Foundation Florida
1–800–879–5400

Someone in this office will ask for your zip code. This person will give you a phone number in your local area, so you can call and inquire about volunteer organizations.

There may be a Volunteer Center in your community. If so, you will be given its number.

Volunteer Center in Your Area

Check your local phone book.

The person in this office will ask you about your interests, where you live, and your age. You will then be referred to one or more local agencies which need your particular skills or interests.

Youth Volunteer Corps of America

Check your local phone book.

This is a national organization with offices in twenty-three cities around the country. They are adding more offices all the time. They will help you start a Youth Volunteer Corps in your community. They work with schools, religious groups, or any organizations that use volunteers. They enable youths eleven to eighteen years of age, to work as a team.

The Youth Volunteer Corps of America helps with housing repair, tutoring, and meal and food distribution.

Volunteer jobs vary, depending on your age and ability. For example, you might help pick up wood, nails, etc. on a house repair project. A young volunteer might help clear the tables after a meal or help prepare food at a soup kitchen. A volunteer of driving age might pick up donated food.

The youth Volunteer Corps of America also acts as a clearing house for other agencies.

The United Way

Check your local phone book.

Your local United Way office should have a Volunteer Center that can refer you to various agencies that need volunteers.

APPENDIX

WHO
WHAT
WHEN
WHERE
WHY

THE NEIGHBORHOOD COALITION
AGAINST HOMELESSNESS

INVITES YOU TO A

STREET FAIR

DATE HERE

ADDRESS HERE

ALL PROCEEDS WILL BE USED FOR
PROGRAMS THAT HELP THE
HOMELESS

❖ SAMPLE PETITION FORM ❖

DATE

To:

We the undersigned ask that:

Signature	Print Name	Your *Address or School* and its address

❖ SAMPLE LETTER FORM ❖

Your Name
Your Address or School and its address
City, State, ZIP

Date

Name of Person To Whom You Are Writing
Title of Person
Name of Organization or Company
Street Address and floor or suite number
City, State, ZIP

Dear (Name):

Text of your letter.

Sincerely,

Your Name
Your Grade

GLOSSARY

advocate One who pleads the cause of another, and defends this cause by argument.

funds Sums of money.

federal funds Sums of federal government money.

official One who holds a position of trust; civil, military, or religious.

petition A formal written request sometimes signed by many people.

poorhouse A public shelter for needy or dependent people.

refugees People who flee to a foreign country to escape danger or persecution.

social welfare Organized public or private social services for the needy.

soup kitchen A lunch room where needy people receive free meals (often soup and bread).

United Nations The international organization of more than 125 nations formed in 1945. The U.N. headquarters is in New York City. Among other things, the U.N. seeks to maintain world peace and security through international cooperation.

volunteers People who offer service of their own free will.

FOR FURTHER READING

Beckelman, Laurie. *The Homeless.* New York: Crestwood House, 1989.

Berck, Judith. *No Place To Be.* Boston: Houghton Mifflin Co., 1992.

DeSoto, Carole. *For Fun and Funds.* West Nyak, NY: Parker Publishing Co., 1983.

Gay, Kathlyn. *Care and Share: Teenagers and Volunteerism.* New York: Simon & Schuster, 1977.

Greenberg, Keith Elliot. *Erik Is Homeless.* Minneapolis, MN: Lerner Publications Co., 1992.

Hauser, Pierre N. *Illegal Aliens.* New York: Chelsea House, 1990.

Johnson, Joan J. *Kids Without Homes.* New York: Franklin Watts, 1991.

Landau, Elaine. *The Homeless.* New York: Simon & Schuster, Inc., 1987.

Lewis, Barbara A. *The Kid's Guide To Social Action.* Minneapolis, MN: Free Spirit Publishing Inc., 1991.

O'Connor. *Homeless Children.* San Diego, CA: Lucent Books, 1989.

ORGANIZATIONS TO CONTACT

The President of the United States
The White House Office
1600 Pennsylvania Ave.
Washington, D.C. 20500

Vice President of the United States
Old Executive Office Bldg.
Washington, D.C. 20501

**Department of Housing and Urban
Development (HUD)**
451 Seventh Street, SW
Washington, D.C. 20410

Department of Health and Human Services
200 Independence Ave., SW
Washington, D.C. 20201

Department of Veteran Affairs
810 Vermont Avenue, NW
Washington, D.C. 20420

**National Network of Runaway and Youth
    Services, Inc.**
1400 I Street, NW
Washington, D.C. 20005

Homelessness Information Exchange
1830 Connecticut Ave., NW, 4th Floor
Washington, D.C. 20009

National Coalition for the Homeless
1612 K Street NW, #1004
Washington, D.C. 20006

National Alliance to End Homelessness, Inc.
1518 K Street NW, Suite 350
Washington, D.C. 20005

CARE
Worldwide Headquarters
660 First Ave.
New York, NY 10016

American Red Cross
Program and Services Department
431 18th Street, NW,
Washington, D.C. 20006

American Red Cross Disaster Relief
PO Box 37243
Washington, D.C. 20013

American Refugee Committee (ARC)
2344 Nicollet Ave., Suite 350
Minneapolis, MN 55404

Habitat for Humanity, International
121 Habitat Street
Americus, GA 31709

Salvation Army
Contact your local chapter, listed in the phone book

**United Nations International Children's
  Emergency Fund (UNICEF)**
3 U.N. Plaza
New York, NY 10017

United Nations Disaster Relief Fund
Secretariat Bldg., Room 2395
One U.N. Plaza
New York, NY 10017

United Way
701 N. Fairfax St.
Alexandria, VA 22314

Mega-Cities
New York, NY 10010

INDEX

ABOUT THE AUTHORS

Eugene Hurwitz earned a B.S. degree in business at the University of Kansas. He works as a commodity trader. He also teaches classes in market theory.

Sue Hurwitz holds an MA in Education from the University of Missouri. She has taught every grade, K-9. Sue is the coauthor of *Drugs and Your Friends, Hallucinogens, Drugs and Birth Defects*, and *Applications: A Guide to Filling Out All Kinds of Forms*.

PHOTO CREDITS: AP/Wide World Photos
PHOTO RESEARCH: Vera Amadzadeh
DESIGN: Kim Sonsky